Draw what you think a TV of the future will look like.
What kinds of programs will be shown?

Create a spaceship. Which galaxy is it in?

These scientists have discovered a prehistoric creature in ice. What does it look like? How old is it?

Draw a city on another planet. Who lives there?

7

Draw all of the players in this soccer game.
Who scores the first goal?

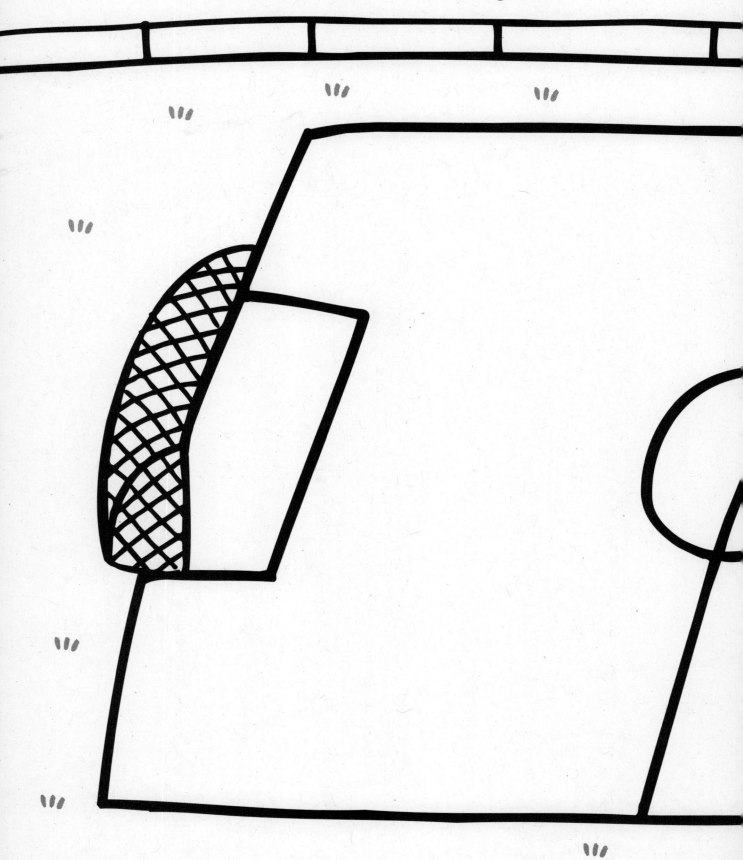

Draw the players on this tennis court. Who wins the match?

11

Design a bridge to help these children cross the river.

Draw the gymnasts in this gymnasium.

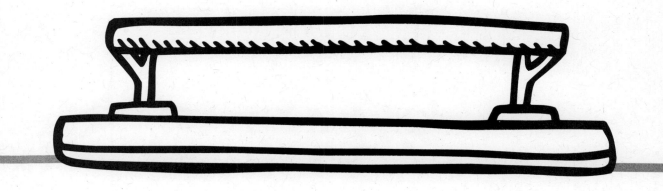

Draw the riders in this horse race.

What masterpiece has this chef created?
What ingredients did he use to make it?

What is under this lamp? Why does it need light?

Draw a family portrait. If you have space, add your friends to the portrait.

Who is on the beach? What are they doing?

Draw an ocean liner in the sea. What does it have on it? Where is it going?

Draw a jungle setting for these animals.

24

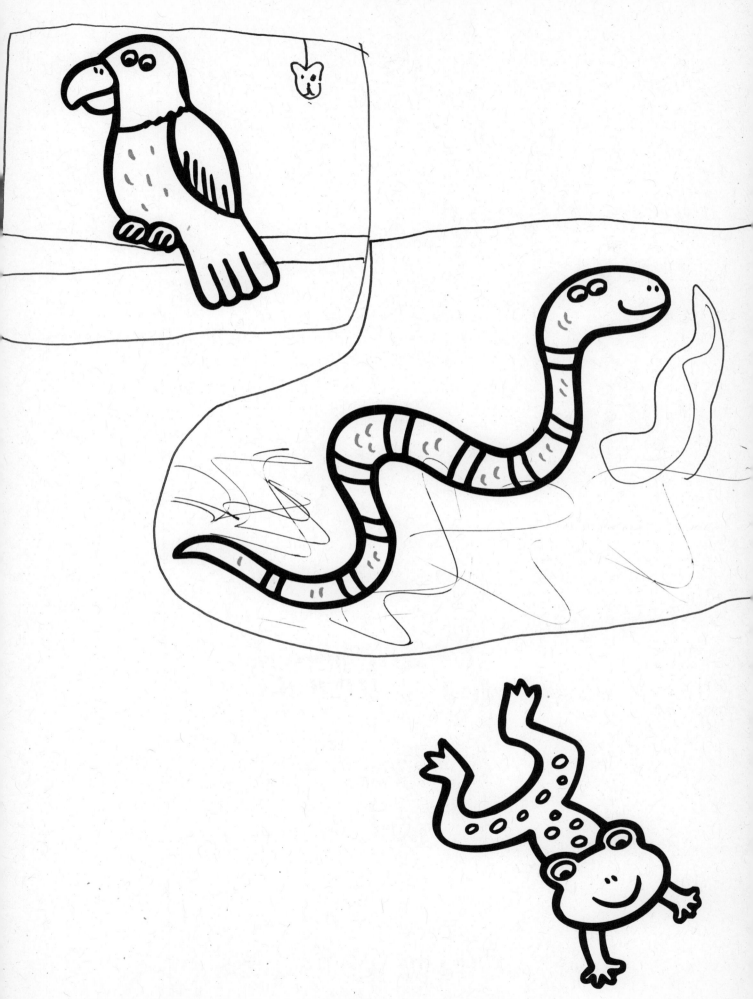

Draw vegetables growing in this garden. What kinds of plants are in the pots?

What is in this store window?

This girl and this boy have just returned from their shopping trip. What is in the bags?

Draw people enjoying this fair.

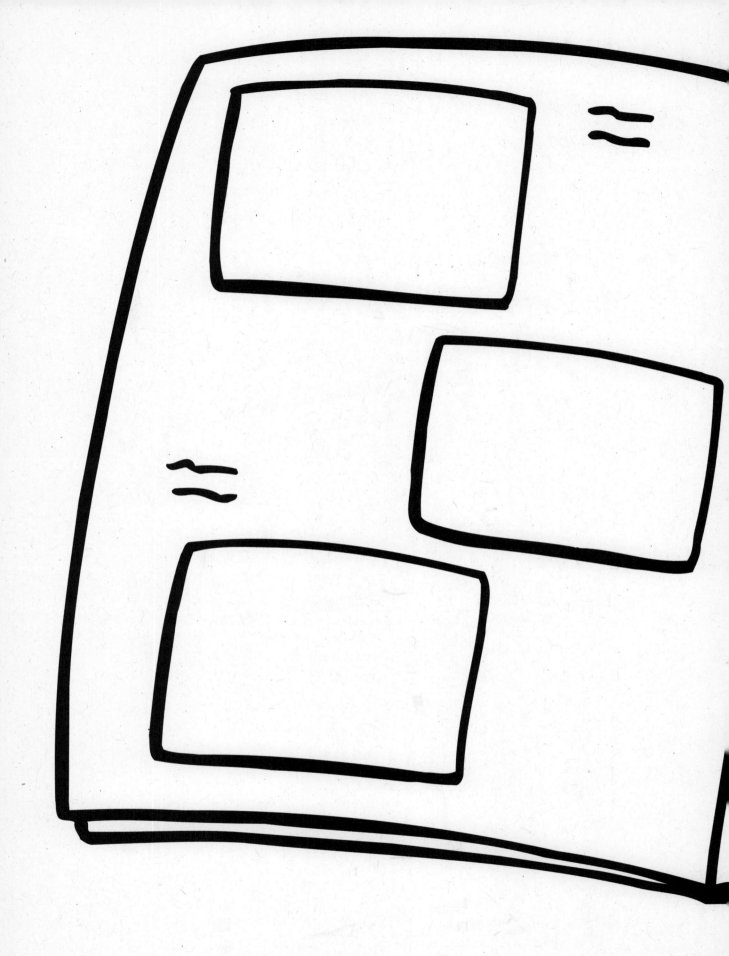

What pictures are in this photo album?

Who is in the airplane? Where are they going? What do the people see below?

What did Farmer John find in his field?

Design a house of the future.

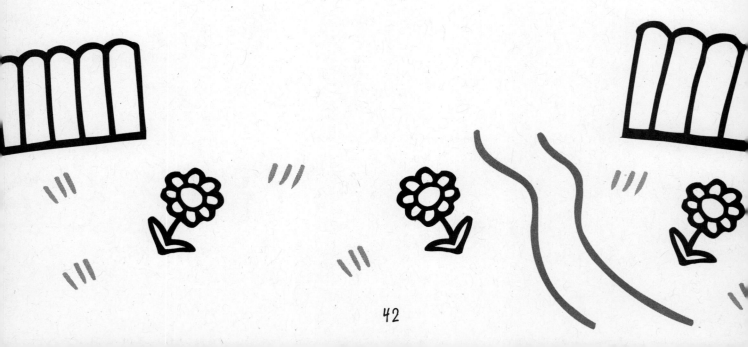

Give this tower a clock. What time is it?

45

What did these men catch on their fishing trip?

Design a beautiful party dress for this young lady.

47

What kinds of animals visited this city last night?

What is living in this tree?

Draw a lighthouse on this cliff.

51

What has this wrestler just won?

Give these actors costumes and props. What play are they in?

Who is in the waves? What are they riding on?

You have been stranded on a desert island.
What do you think you will need?

What is at the end of this spooky path?

Whom should this player pass the ball to?

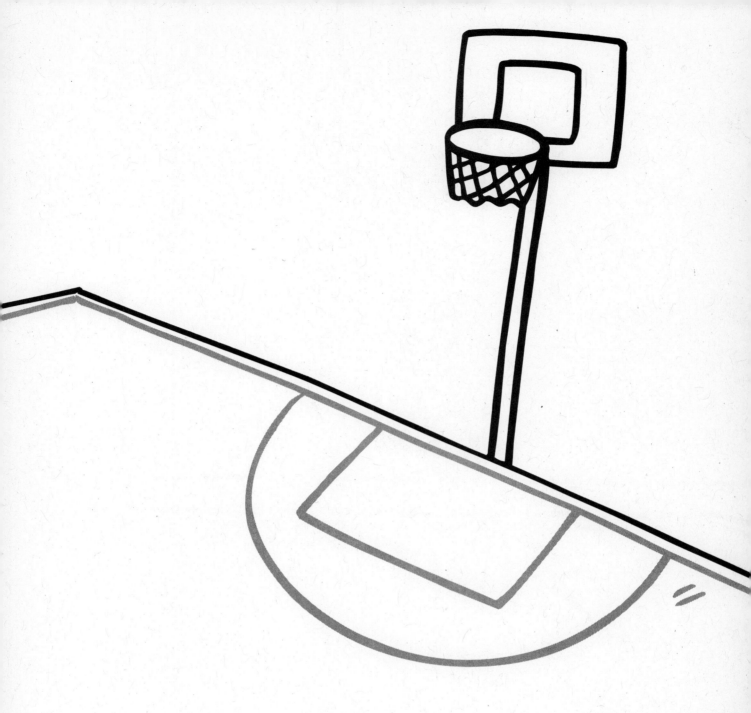

Who is hurrying to buy the last cupcake?

What is being served in this cafeteria?

Draw a crew to help this captain.

Draw a conductor for this orchestra.

Who is going up in this hot air balloon?

Draw a silly container for these flowers.

Draw the owner of this hat.

Draw a house made of different types of candy.
Who lives there?

This room is a mess! Draw a robot to clean it up.

What is outside of this bedroom window?

Draw some constellations in the sky. What are the names of the constellations?

What do these children see out of their car windows?

75

What treasures lie at the bottom of this ocean?

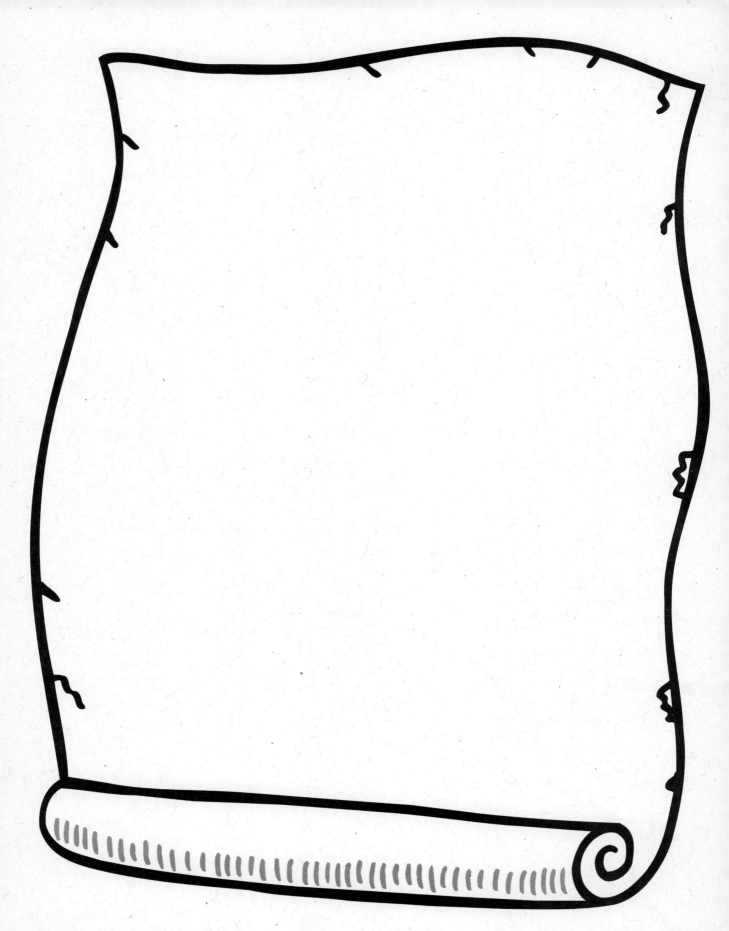

Draw a map of your house. Where will you hide your treasure? Mark your hiding place with an X.

What type of boat are these children paddling?
Where are they?

What do you imagine that these people are thinking?

What woke up these people?

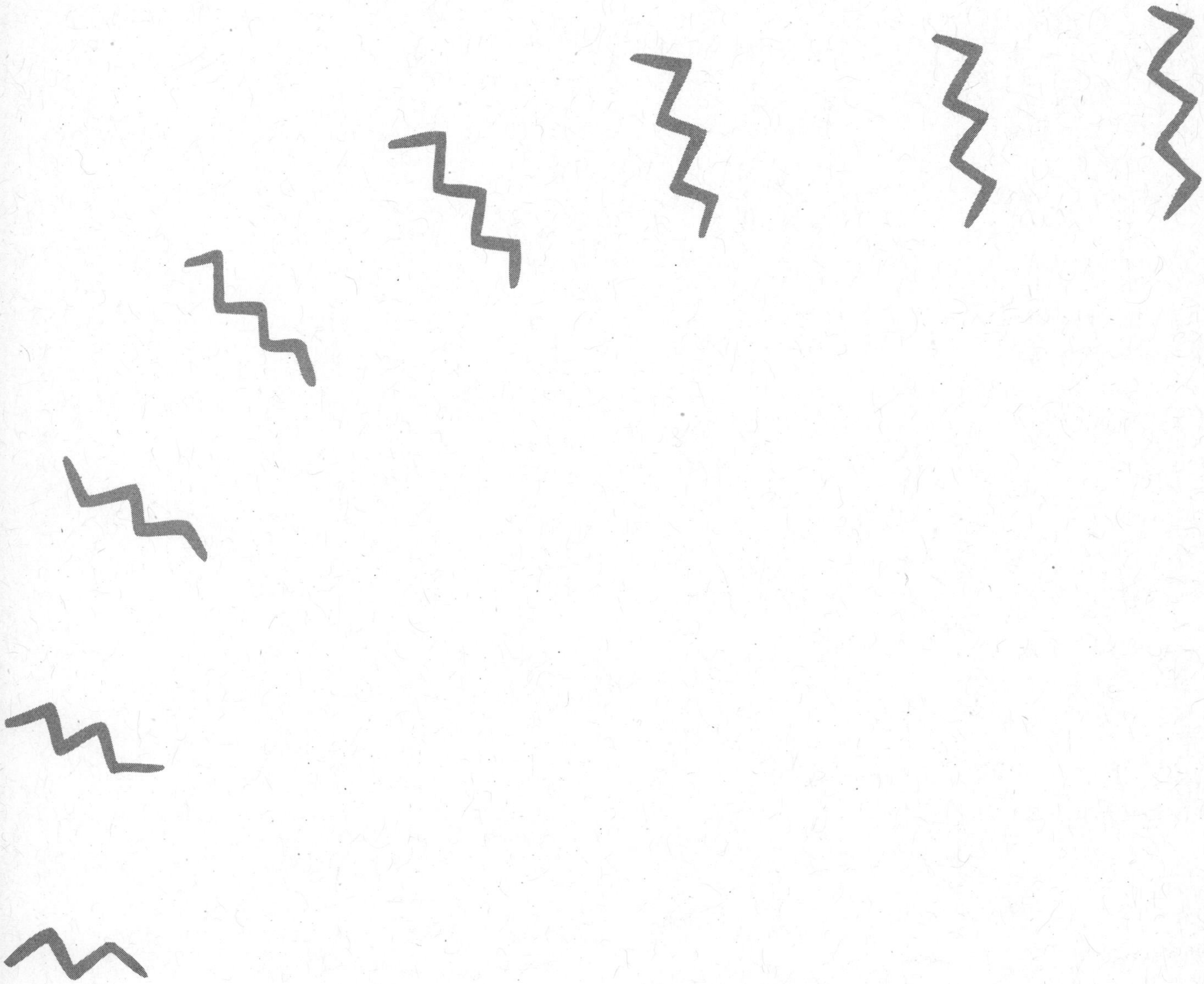

Your favorite video game is on the computer screen.
What does it look like?

Draw the girl's reflection in the mirror.

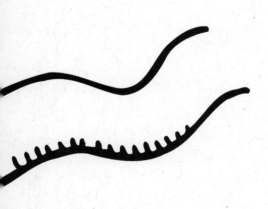

Help this mother rabbit go down the rabbit hole to her babies. Draw the connecting tunnels.

Who else is skating in the rink?

Oh no! Professor Igor has combined two creatures.
What does his new creature look like?

What are these campers missing?

Draw what you would wish for if you were granted three wishes.

This boy found a magical old lamp and is polishing it. What happens next?

These people are going to a costume party.
Draw detailed masks for them.

You have discovered a new type of underwater creature. What does it look like?

Decorate this tour bus for your favorite musical group.

95

Design the super car of tomorrow.

What has this scientist invented?

97

Design a MISSING poster for Corky the cocker spaniel.

Design some new coins. What pictures are on them?

This cave hasn't been lived in for years. Who lived there

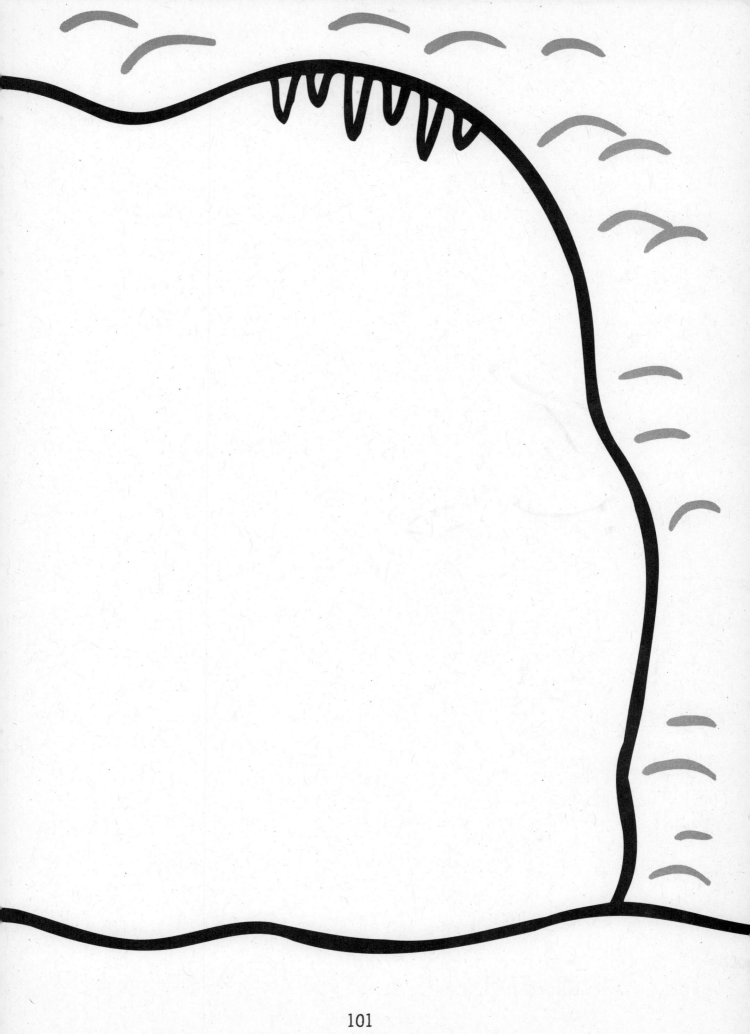

Complete this prehistoric scene.

What has this archaeologist discovered in her backyard?

Draw this girl's masterpiece.

What is beyond the gate in this mysterious garden?

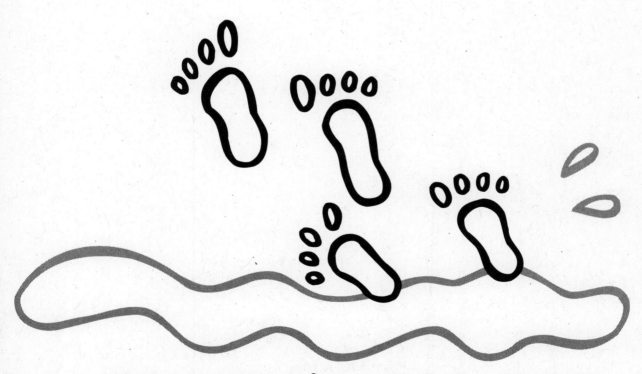

Whom do these footprints belong to?

Design a rocket to take you to outer space.
What will you take with you?

Draw a bowling ball that will help you get a strike.

Who lives on this planet?

Help the ant find his friends. Draw the connecting tunnels.

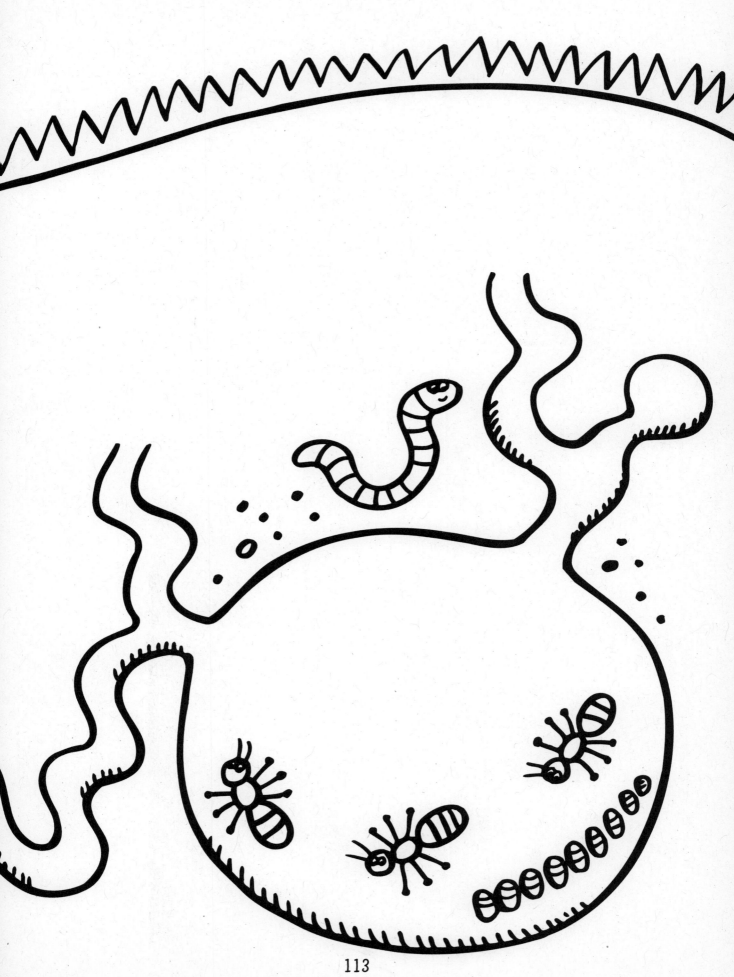

113

What is on the space transporter?

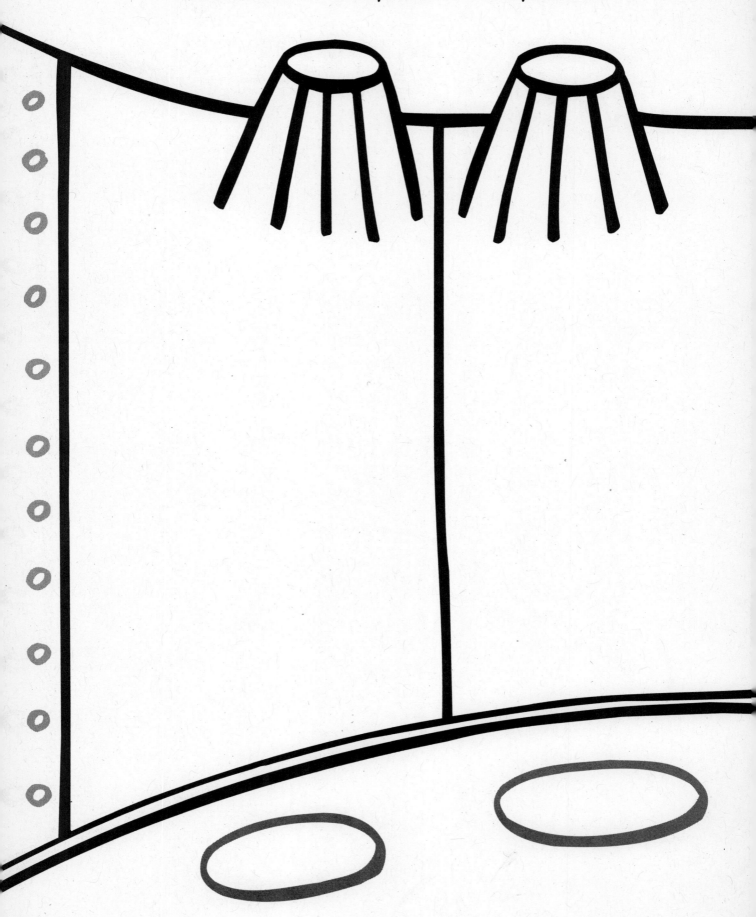

Fill this botanical garden.

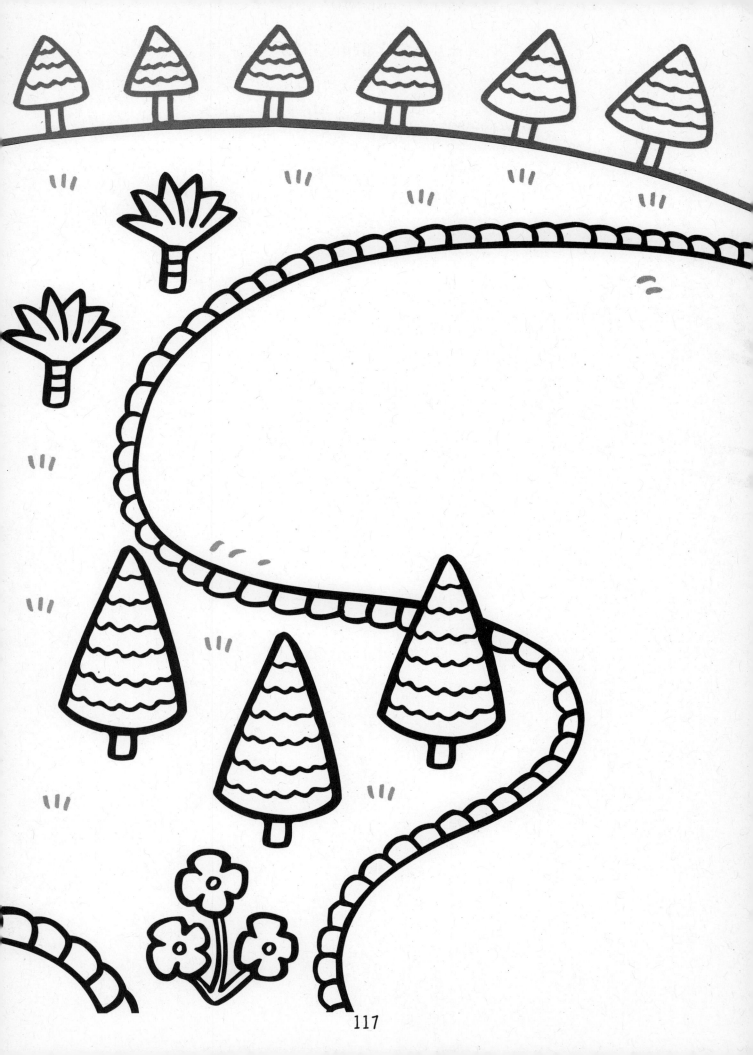

Draw the engine in this car.

Oh no! Professor Igor has done it again!
Which two creatures has he combined this time?
What does this new creature look like?

119

Complete these pipelines.

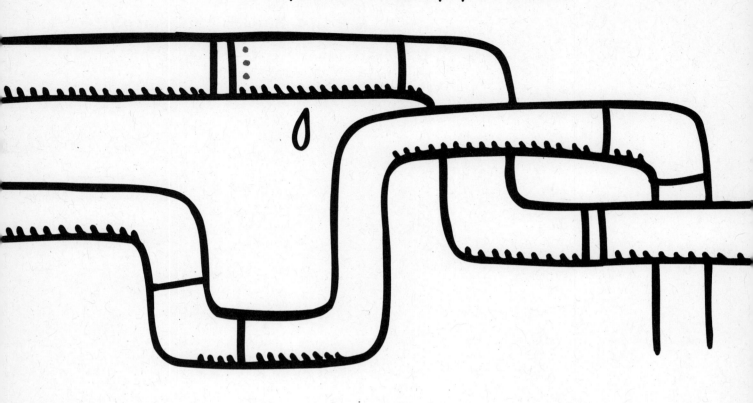

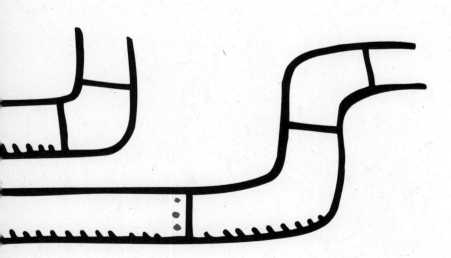

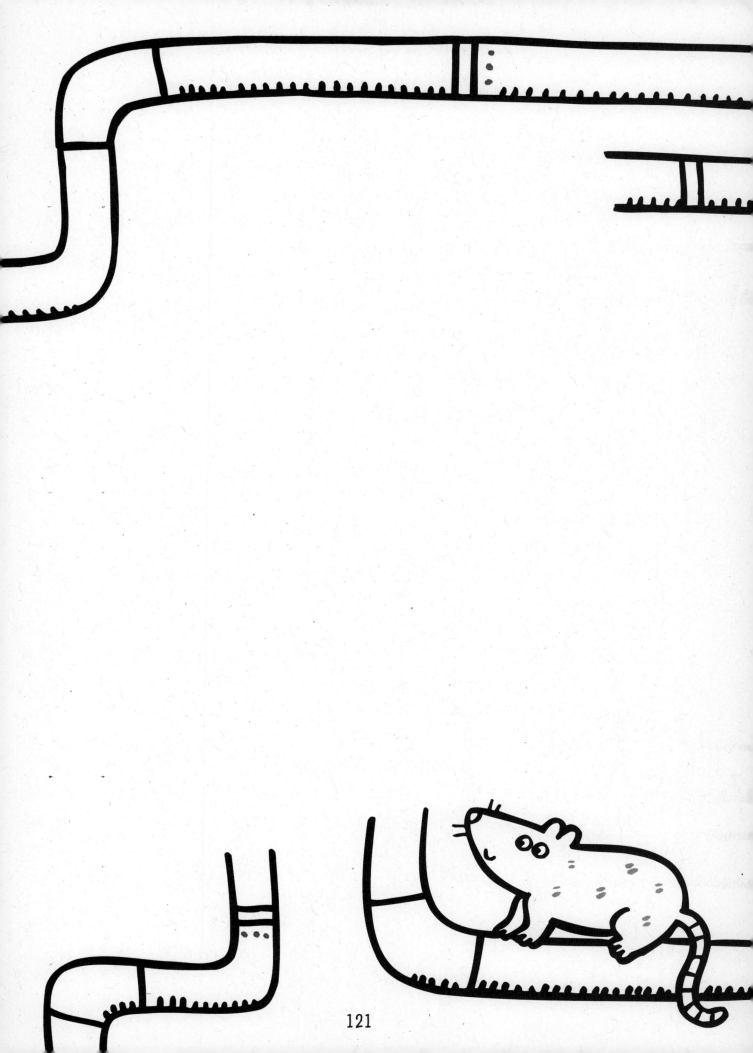

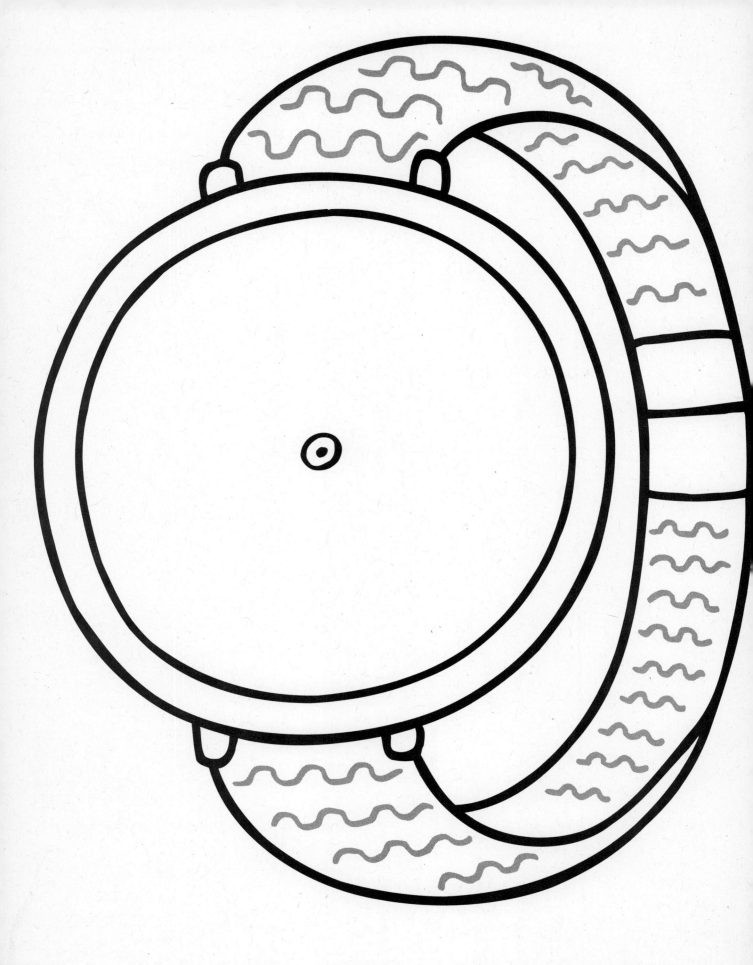

Design the watch face. What time is it?

Draw a shipwreck at the bottom of the ocean.
What has made a home in it?

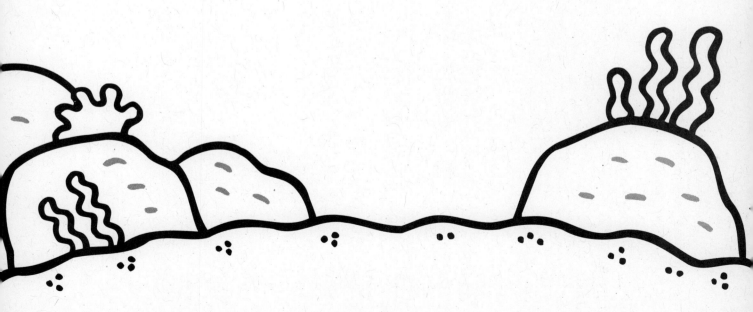

What does this man see in the desert?

Draw a house for these birds.

125

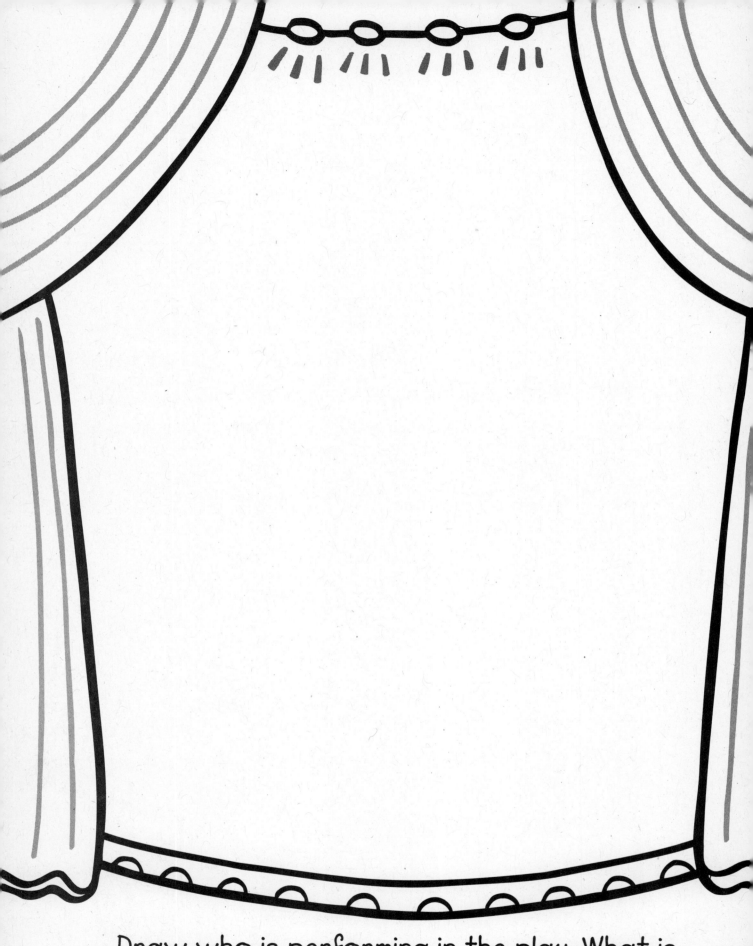

Draw who is performing in the play. What is the play about?

Imagine that you are an architect. Draw a house for a mouse.

Imagine that you are an explorer. You have just discovered a new species of bird. What does it look like?

What is this racer riding?

Draw the **monster** that has destroyed this town.

Design a menu for a space café.

MENU

This birthday present is for you! What is in the box?

ipad toch

Who is skiing in this downhill race? Who will win?

Decorate this shield for a knight in armor.

Draw skateboarders doing tricks on the ramp.

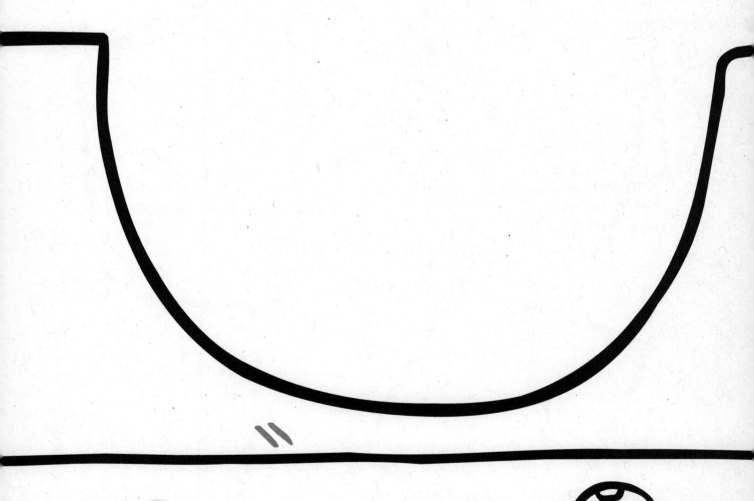

Design a new set of postage stamps. What pictures are on them?

A famous sculptor has run out of ideas for his masterpiece. Help him by drawing your own sculpture.

Draw a statue of the school mascot
in front of this school.

Clark has invented a machine that makes 100 doughnuts per minute. What does it look like?

What are these sisters thinking of eating for breakfast?

This girl is trying to catch the strangest bug in the world! What does it look like?

Secret Agent James Blonde has a gadget that captures bad guys. How does it work? What does it look like?

Design a city of the future. What changes will there be?

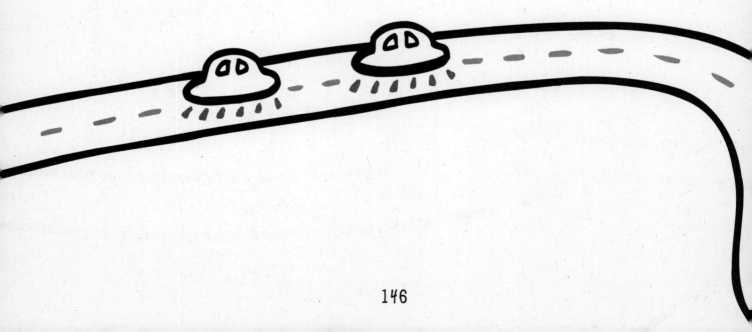

Vroom! Vroom! Draw another car in this race.

You are shopping for a party. What items are in your shopping bag?

This dog is in a dog show. Draw the other contestants and their owners. Who won first, second, and third prize?

150

This sheriff is putting up WANTED posters for Big Bad Ben. Ben is wanted for eating homework. What does Ben look like? Draw him on the poster.

WANTED

Alfred the wizard has used a magic spell to conjure up a dragon. What kind of dragon is it? Does it breathe fire?

James Blonde needs a super-duper spy car for his latest mission. Design one that has plenty of gadgets.

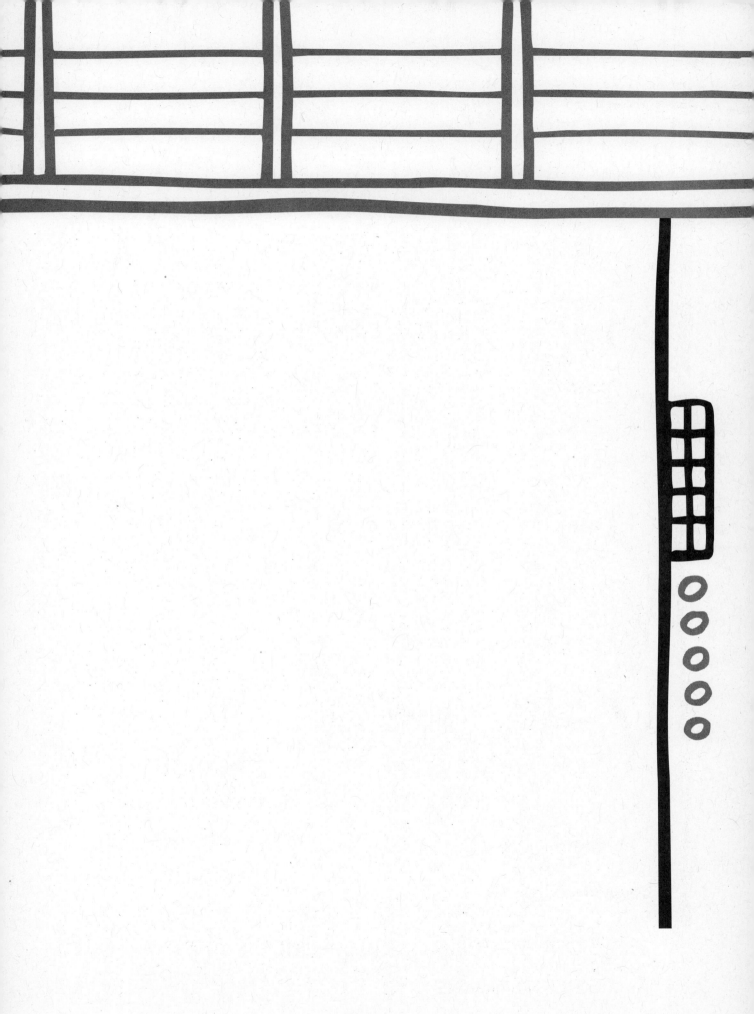

Draw something that will scare away the crows.

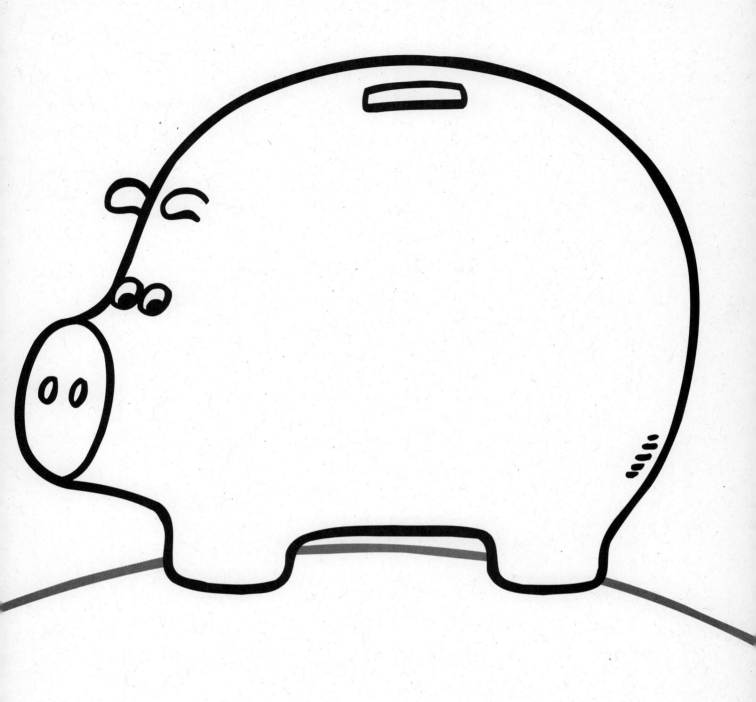

What is inside the piggy bank?

Draw a picture of your pet
or a pet you would like to have.

Dress this young lady for a princesses' ball.

Draw a magical beanstalk growing up to the cloud. Who is climbing the beanstalk?

Turn this chair into a throne fit for a king or a queen.

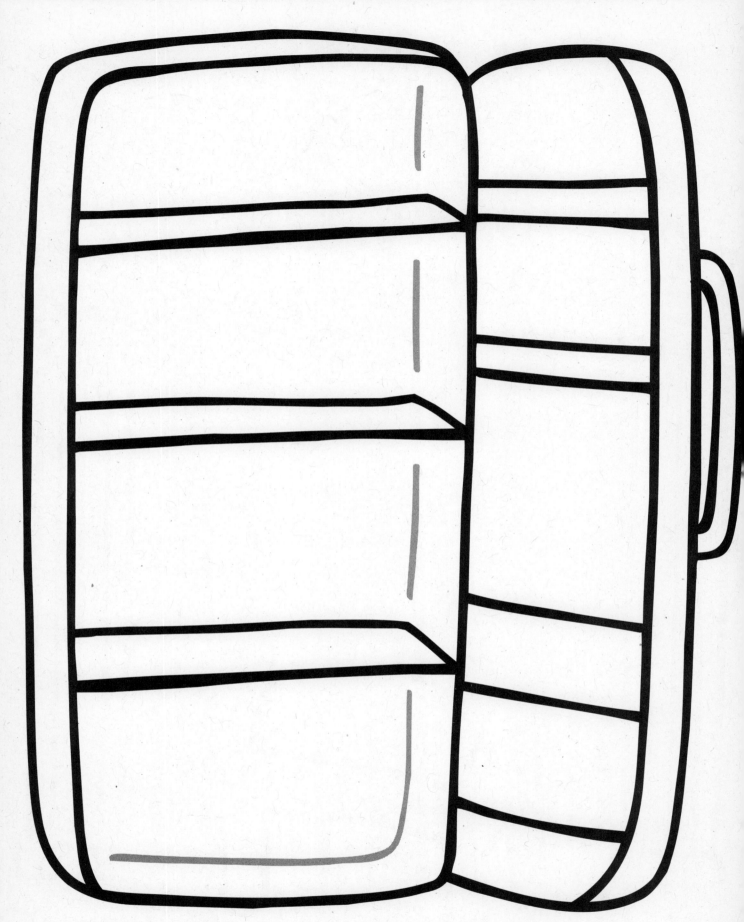

Fill this refrigerator with your favorite things to drink and eat.

Draw the front cover of your favorite book.

Draw the characters from your favorite TV show.

What has this boy created?

Draw a picture of you and your best friend.

What has hatched from this egg?

Draw your dream tree house.

Betsy Brianna is designing a new backpack just for you. Can you help her?

Give these women wacky hairstyles.

This diver has found a beautiful coral reef filled with sea life. What does it look like?

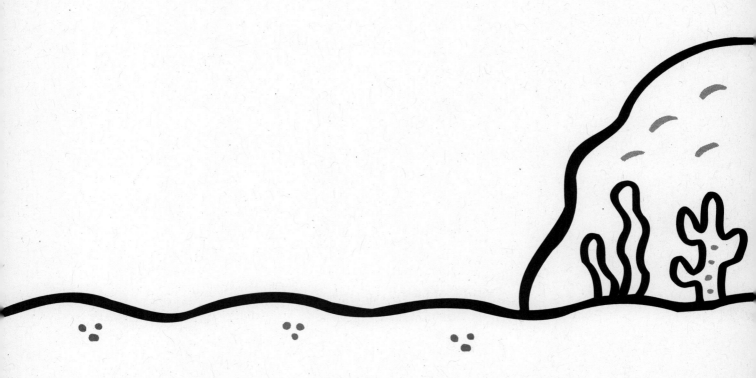

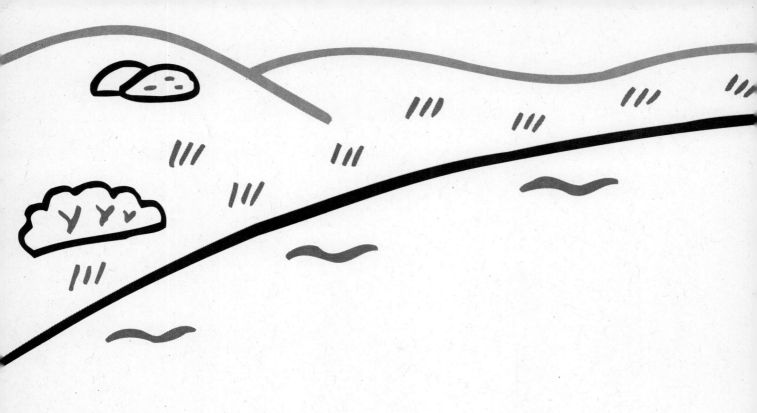

You have spotted the Loch Ness monster.
What does it look like?

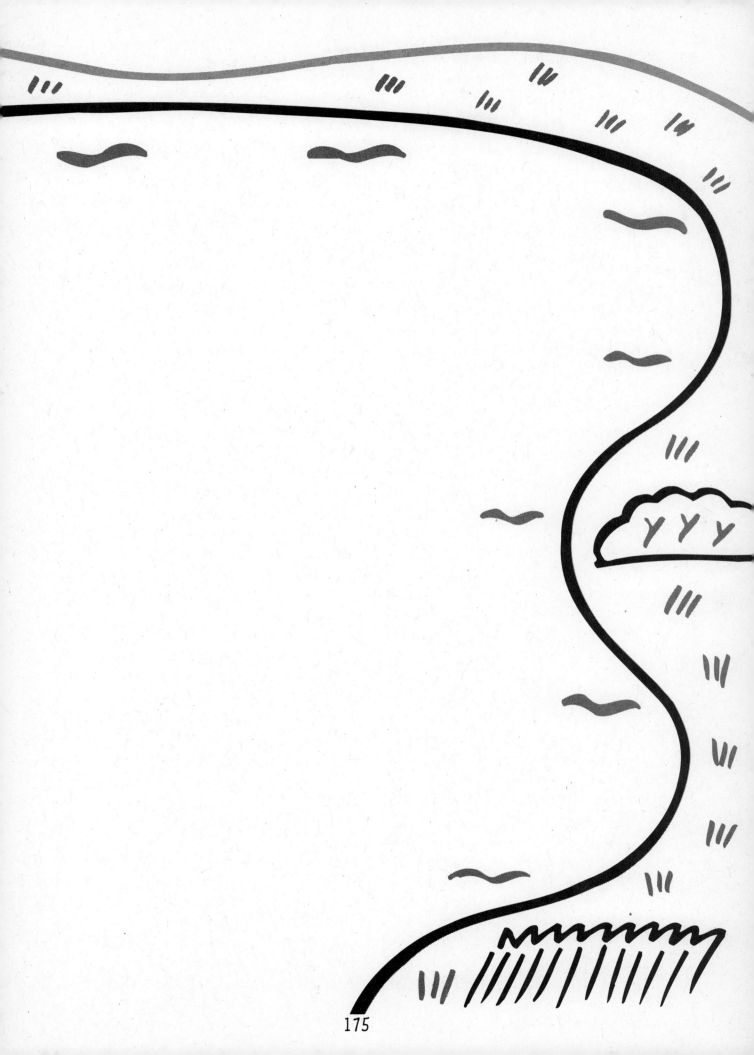

Draw the Abominable Snowman in this snowy scene.

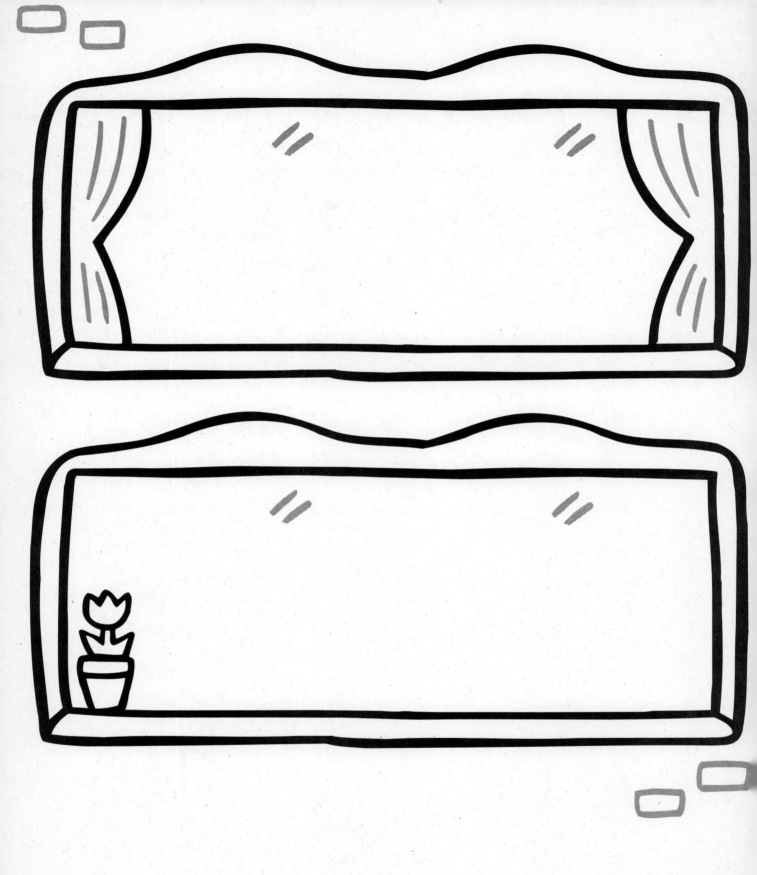

The cat is meowing and keeping everyone awake.
Draw the people in the windows. How do they look?

Design a MISSING poster for Winnie the guinea pig.

MISSING

Draw a clown for this party.

Draw yourself standing on the top step of the podium. What did you win first prize for?

Draw you and your family going on a trip somewhere.
How will you get there?

Turn this garden into a winter wonderland.

185

Draw some neighbors in this apartment building.
What are they doing?

Who is next to the pool? Who is in the pool?

Draw some space friends for the astronaut.

What do you see on the ground, in the trees,
and in the night sky?

Why is this man running?

You have landed on a strange, new planet.
Complete the scene.

Design new soccer uniforms for this team. Give each player's jersey a different number.

Who is riding the bus? Where is it going?

Draw airplanes performing at this air show.

Draw a monster truck driving over these three cars.

What lives under this bridge?

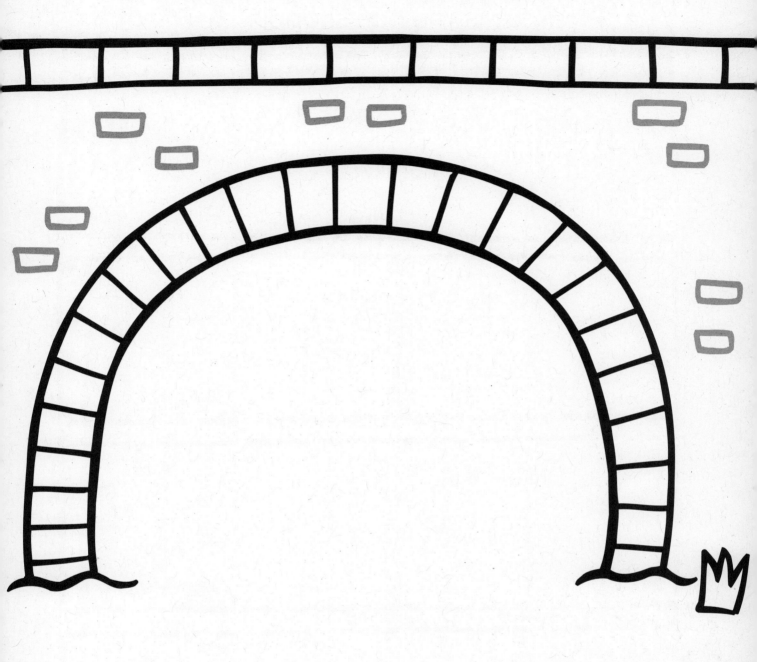

What is missing from the shelves of this store?
What is the man shopping for?

What has cowboy Clint caught using his amazing lasso-handling skills?

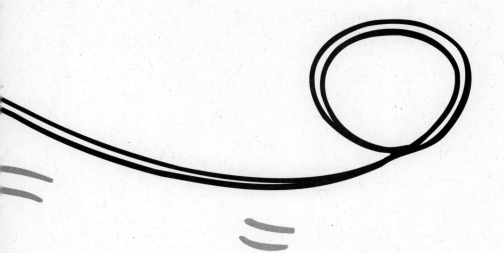

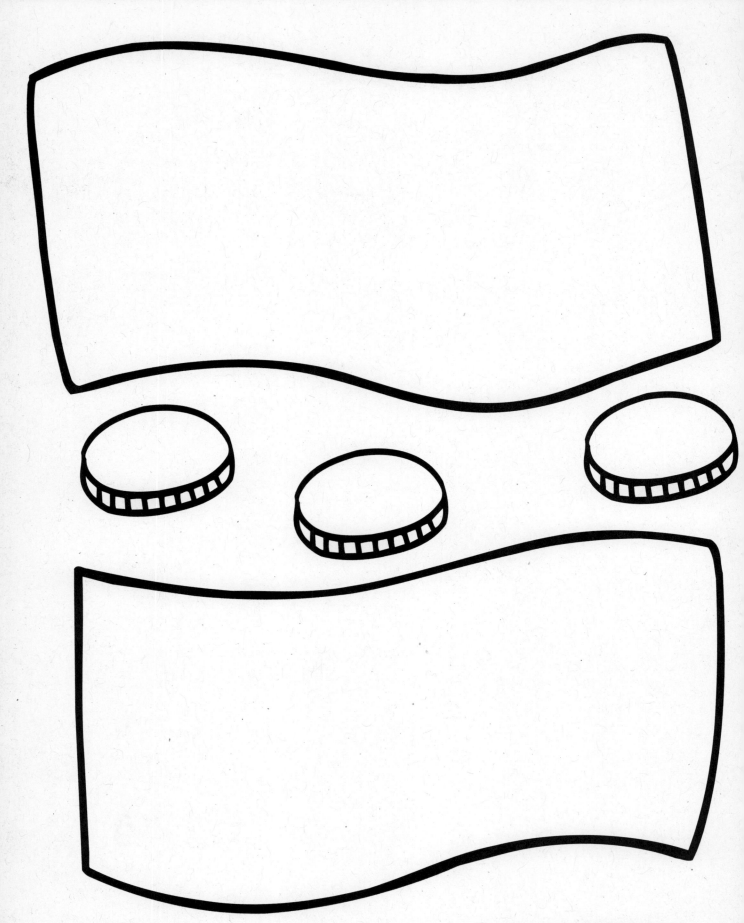

You have uncovered an old pirate chest filled with money. What does the money look like?

What has the archaeologist found in this case?

207

What has just been teleported into this space station?

Reporter Sid Snoop is trying to get a news interview. Who is he trying to interview?

Draw a detailed map of where Captain Crabb hid his treasure.

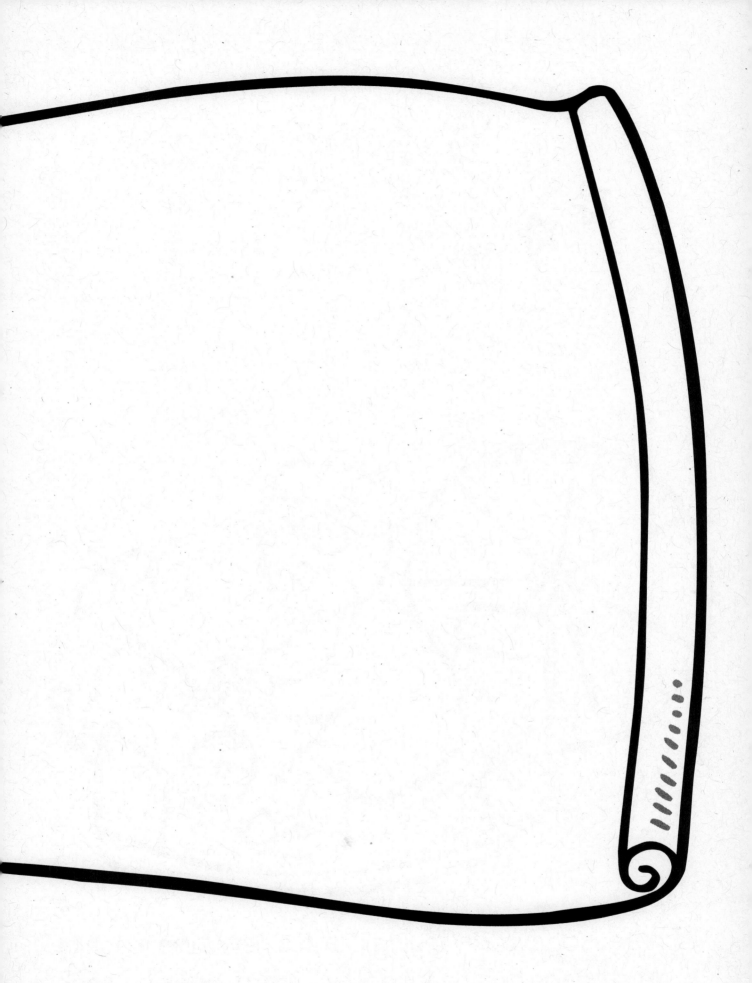

211

Professor Ivan is trying out his new time machine. What year has he landed in? What does he see?

Fill this photo album with pictures of places you would love to visit.

Fill this museum with a collection of art.

Draw this family's home.

219

Draw the haunted house that this salesperson just visited.

Draw a crown of jewels on display.

This archaeologist has discovered a hidden temple that has not been seen for thousands of years. What does it look like?

223

This wildlife photographer has been waiting patiently for an unusual animal to walk into view. No one has ever seen this animal before. What does it looks like?

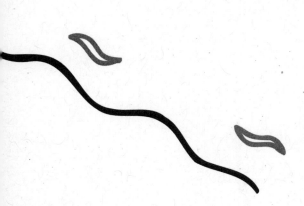

Design a boat to take you down this river.

Rocket Starjet is chasing an alien spacecraft through the galaxy. Draw the alien spacecraft and give it a name.

What is growing in this field? What is missing from
this farm scene?

What lives in this desert?

What lives in this rain forest?

What lives in this African savannah?

What are the children eating at their picnic
on the beach?

Imagine that you are a super-whiz on the computer. Design your own web site. What will be on it?

This newspaper contains your school news. Give the newspaper a name. What stories and pictures are in the news today?

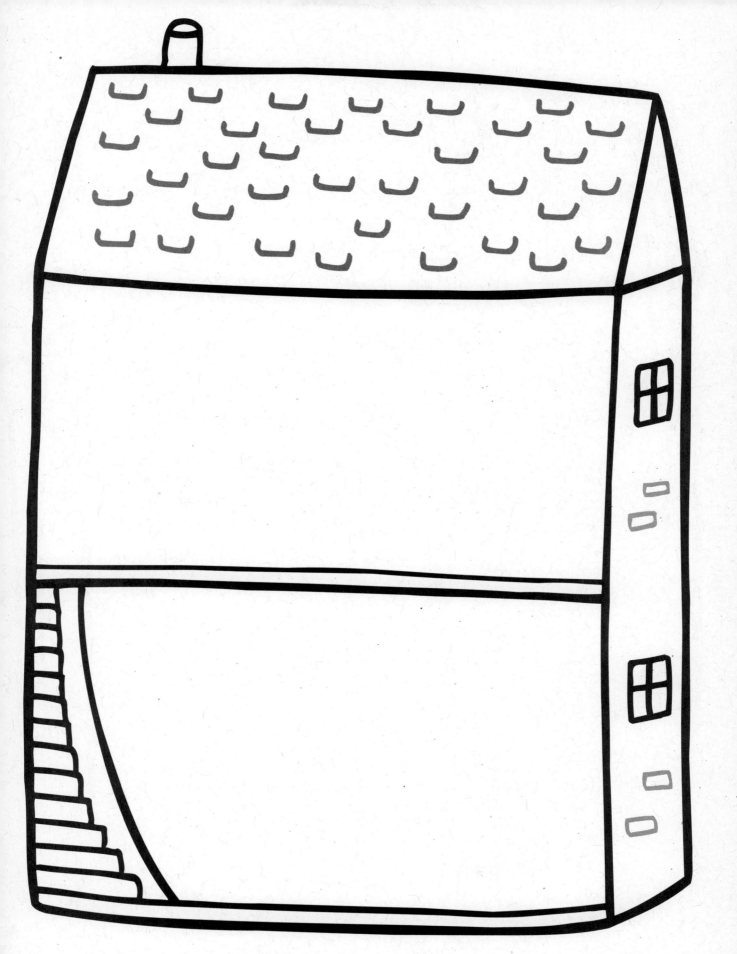

Furnish this dollhouse.

Who or what is hiding under the bed?

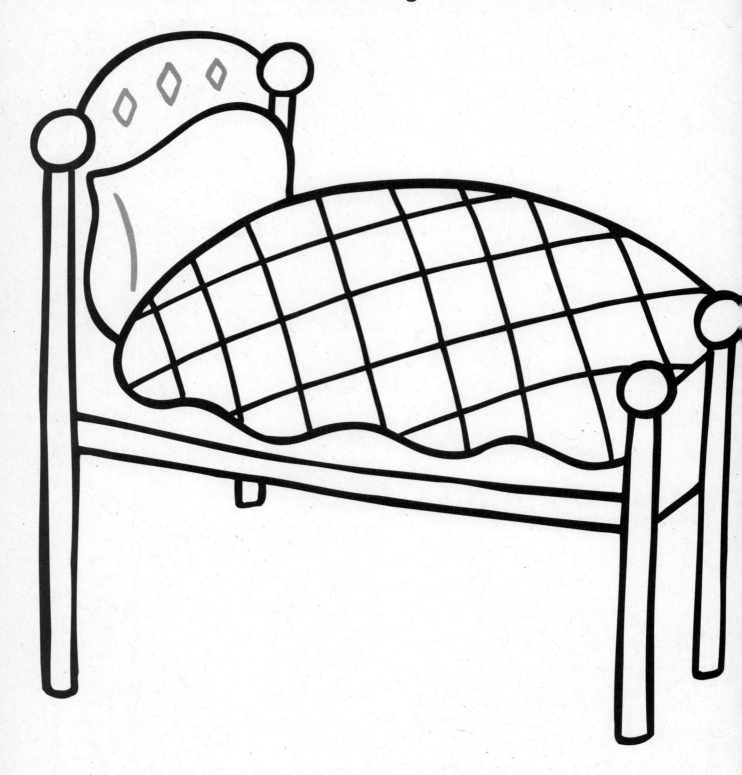

Whom do these nuts belong to?

What type of animal is grazing by the watering hole?

Draw a playground for these children to play in.

What is interested in the flowers?

What lives in this polar region?

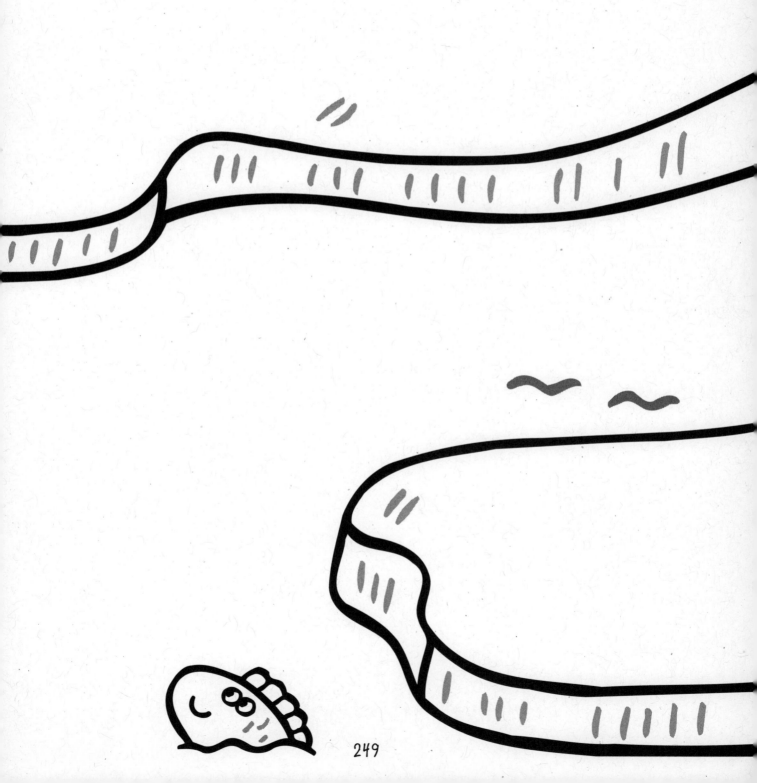

249

Who is at this party? What are they doing?

What do you see in this pond?

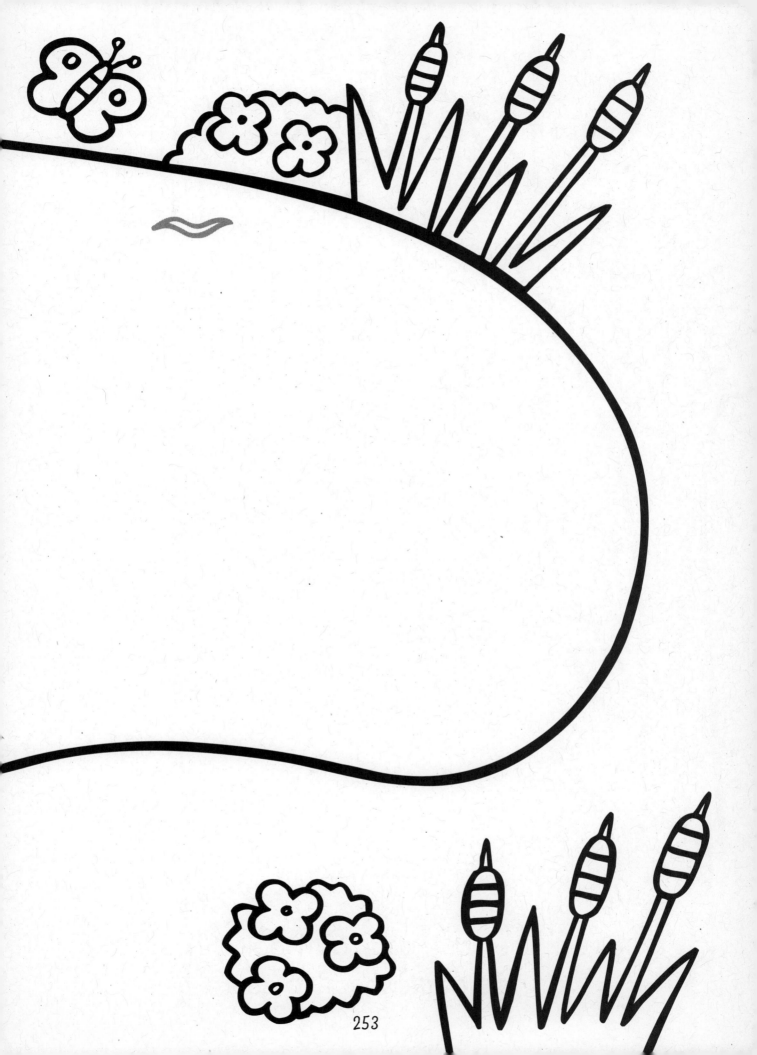

253

You are in the Australian outback. What animals do you expect to see?